the Eagle
and the Butterfly

Interpretation of the Apostle Paul's
teachings were gratefully accepted
from Wayne F. Barnes.

Cover illustration and interior sketches
created by Patti Reeder Eubank.

the Eagle
and the Butterfly

by Mary Moline

A Mary Moline Publication of
Green Valley World, Inc.
41 South Ocean Avenue
Cayucos, California 93430

This book is a first edition
2000 copies printed in March, 1986.

ISBN: 0-913444-10-3

Printed in the United States of America

If We Live By The Spirit
Let Us Also Be Directed By The Spirit

Galations 5:25

CHAPTER ONE

Not far from Santa Barbara, a fruitful emerald valley opens southward to the sea. The gentle, fertile hills rise to the north and east to form the Santa Ynez Mountains. It is from a tree that clings to those high craggy cliffs that a bald eagle protects his domain. He awakens as the purple softness of the early morning sun intrudes into his eight-foot nest of grass, leaves and limbs. He feels uncomfortable but does not know why. The eagle is aroused and instinctively repelled when he realizes that an unwelcome visitor dares to spend the night in the lofty comfort of his nest. His gray feathers ruffle and he snaps his yellow beak in a noisy, nervous rhythm. He grows angry and wild with rage. He assumes an attitude of attack. He silences the intruder, then shakes his feathers to rid himself of the awareness of a disturbed nature. Like a man desperately in love, he cherishes and guards the things that are rightfully his.

The confident eagle settles back into his nest and begins to glance at his immediate surroundings. He is quick to realize there is another intruder to his lair. The feathers at the back of his neck stand on end, and the usual softness in his eyes switches to a golden glare. He does not move. He is hypnotised by the aura of the panorama before him. The vision he sees holds him frozen. A fragile Monarch Butterfly emerges from a filmy golden-green crystalline pouch on a branch below. The eagle has seen this sight before, but never on his mountain. The awareness of her birth leaves him disturbed. He fights to maintain his composure. He sinks his talons deep into his perch. The bewildered bird rolls his head, first from one side, then to the other. He tries to grasp the reality of the lowly butterfly having the audacity to be born on his mountain.

"What are you doing here?" he thunders.
"You belong down in the valley with the
others! You have no place on my mountain!"

The new-born butterfly breathes fullness into her limp body and spreads her wings to dry in the sunshine before she answers.

"You dare to ask, to know? My soul is
empty. I seek oneness to fill it."

"Oneness?" he laughs. "'There are
millions of butterflies and you seek oneness?"

With complete confidence, she answers,

"Certainly! The oneness I seek is much
more than being alone."

The magnificent eagle is taken aback by the butterfly's honesty. His voice cracks as he mutters,

"Oneness is all I've known since I lost
my mate."

The butterfly does not listen to his heart-felt words.

"The oneness I seek is of mind, feeling
and free spirit. You might call it 'freedom.'"

Displeased by her insensitivity, he rips a sheath of bark from the tree with his talons.

"I call it trespassing!" he blunders.

The delicate motion of the butterfly fanning her sun-shot wings holds the eagle's golden eye in a daze.

"Have no fear," she assures him. "I am just the first. There is room for those who follow."

The eagle is amazed at the butterfly's appetite for adventure.

"Why have you set yourself apart from the crowd? You are not equal to reach such heights. It is I, the eagle, who is the image of greatness. You, self-destroying butterfly, as well as those who follow, are born out of the likeness of me."

The aroused bird leaps from branch to branch in a nervous rage. The butterfly tries to stay clear of his erratic movements. After much maneuvering, the eagle settles down on a limb above her. He spreads his giant wings to shade her from the sun. The butterfly flutters to the edge of his nest to escape his shadow.

"Why must you be so unyeilding and inconsiderate? The size of you is shading my growth. Don't you realize that I need the light?"

Her attitude angers him. His body stiffens and his feathers compress. He twists his head in violent circular jerks. He cannot tolerate a butterfly in **his** lair. He thrashes his seven-foot span of wings, sweeping her out of his nest. She is not afraid. She escapes his wrath by drifting upward to a delicate twig at the top of the tree. Bewildered, he stares at her as though in a trance.

For generations millions of Monarchs have migrated through the Owens Valley, over the Sierra Mountains, across the Tehachapis to the Pacific Ocean. That this one butterfly dared to be born on his mountain is more than he can bear.

The eagle's heavily guarded emotion is nurtured by his inborn instinct to protect his domain. This is the only home he has known. He has shared his lair with no one since his mate was lost. He chooses to remain alone. The eagle's reason for being is to protect his domain, to leave it is unthinkable. Any intruder into the lair of the eagle will soon realize the fear of his presence.

> "Get out of my tree! Get down from my mountain! You are easily destroyed, butterfly!"

She does not move. She shows no fear. Her determination is equal to his.

The giant Monarch is perplexed by the fragile butterfly. He does not accept her, nor her request for oneness. To encourage her is absurd. He does not understand this meaning of 'oneness.' Nor does he seek to be informed. The need for her kind of achievement is confusing to him. He wonders if he should act or react. Looking deceptively gentle, he examines her, first with one eye, and then, snapping his head to the left, with the other. He is aware she has risen from the plain to his arena, but he chooses not to acknowledge her progress.

"You must leave my tree at once," he orders.

She ignores his command. The butterfly is insensitive to the eagle's wrath because she is moved by forces beyond her control. This is her moment, the moment of realizing the fullest expectation of her desires. Her heart and mind are in awe of the glory of her rebirth.

"Do not worry yourself with me. I will not stay long. I have much to do and my time is short."

The eagle attempts to diminish the butterfly's request by belittling her.

> "You have nothing to do but drink from
> the flowers and drift along with the wind."

For the first time she is aware that this bird is indeed 'unenlightened.'

> "Oh, proud eagle, little you know of
> butterflies. Do not confuse me with the
> moth who would fly into the cobweb, mis-
> directed, to die. Please know that I have
> a destiny, and I will return."

> "Not to my tree!" he screeches.

The Monarch Butterfly is guided, like her ancestors, to retrace her pilgrimage across prairies, deserts, mountain valleys, even cities, to complete her cycle.

> "No, not to your tree but to the side of
> your mountain," she explains.

> "No, not to my mountain!" the defiant
> eagle warns.

His words do not surprise her.

"Your attitude is very negative."

"Negative!" the eagle snaps. "I am not negative, but I am **positive** I don't want you here."

She quickly counters:

"Do not confuse arrogance with positiveness."

"Arrogance? he cries. "Are you not aware that I am the Monarch?"

"Oh, proud eagle, your awareness is limited to the length of your wingspread."

The challenged eagle leaps about on his pearch. He shuffles his wing feathers and brags:

"What are you talking about? I can soar higher and see farther than anyone, for I am Monarch of all I survey."

The butterfly lands on a leaf not more than six inches from the eagle's head. She stares directly into his penetrating golden orbs and insists,

"I, too, am a Monarch."

The eagle laughs at her statement.

"The altitude has gone to your puny brain.
You're not a Monarch, you're merely a wind-
tossed scrap of life, that's what you are!"

The butterfly is saddened by his attitude but continues to plead with the arrogant bird.

"Within me there is a hunger to reach the
one who would recognize my needs. I have
waited for this moment of freedom to share
mutual joy."

The eagle's reaction is electric.

"Now I have heard everything! Your
obsession for freedom is limited to your
drive for self-preservation and security.
Are you not aware of that?"

She shakes her head in response to his rash statement.

"That is not so. I am aware that I was
born in bondage . . . but freedom is my
birthright."

She pauses and wistfully smiles, waiting for his reaction. He says nothing. His feathers remain compressed, and he turns his head away from her.

The butterfly moves her wings in a flashing color of motion as she dances on the branch above him, then continues to speak.

> "I must have freedom to love and be loved.
> I have not taken the impossible flight.
> Because of the worth of pain, and to know
> its magic, I am advanced to a higher arena."

The eagle angrily shakes his feathers and jerks his head in several directions. He cannot bring himself to acknowledge her growth. Instead, he flaps his giant wings and boasts:

> "Rare is the moment of such advancement.
> Only eagles enter such arenas."

The butterfly prances about in the sunshine as its warmth floods though the leaves of the tree. The scales on her wings are like black velvet. She is now ready to continue her journey.

> "Oh, giant bird, of course I do not have
> your energy, but I do have more endurance."

The eagle sputters and coughs. He twists his head and shakes his tail feathers. She has caught him off guard. His words become defensive.

> "I am not like the sacrificing moth drawn
> to destruction in a burning flame," he
> argues.

> "Dear wise eagle, your feelings are buried
> so deep, I wonder if you have the compassion
> to understand me?"

This hurts him. He is reminded of how his compassion was lost on the wings of his mate.

> "I have no time to concern myself with
> feelings. I must look after my domain."

The butterfly asks to be understood, but the eagle pretends not to hear her. He tucks his head under his wing and he makes a clucking sound as she talks.

> "Without reason I was lost. Now that I
> have found myself, I am renewed."

Once more the wounded eagle parries.

> "Do you really know what you want?"

His words become heavy on her heart, and tears well into her eyes.

"Oh, I do," she whispers. "This longing
for 'oneness' has created a spirit of
greater freedom within me, but not everyone
understands."

He deflects her plea for understanding by compressing his feathers while maintaining a solid grip on his perch. He is a stubborn fellow. He would rather do battle with logic than with passion. He is afraid of expressing honest emotion, fearful of the resulting action. He ponders her words. The butterfly drifts away from the tree, then back again.

"You seek freedom," he cries, "but you
don't know what to do with it. What experience do you have?"

Without hesitation, the butterfly answers:

"With enthusiasm, anything is possible."

Now he is truly angry.

"Be gone with you, butterfly! I am the
Monarch of the sky. I have no more time for
your fantasies."

The butterfly flutters to an outside branch to catch the drift of the wind. She is poised, ready to continue her journey. She flies away from the nest; but, almost as though drawn by a magnet, she flies back to him and pauses for a fleeting second on his ruffled neck feathers.

"You are not the only Monarch,"
she whispers.

She then drifts out of sight.

For a long while he circles the lonely sky. She has left him doubtful and perplexed. He is angry with himself but does not know why.

"I will prove that I am the Monarch of the sky, the **only** Monarch!"

CHAPTER TWO

T he eagle's graceful sweep across the sky changes into a purposeful pattern. His giant wings hum against the wind as he begins to quarter in an upward spiral.

"What is the matter with me?" he asks himself. "Have I not flown as high as I might? Must I compete for my place in the sky with a butterfly? To know, I must risk again."

The eagle is not known to falter. He seldom misses his prey, but the encounter with the butterfly has left him uncomfortably bound to her spirit and unsure of himself.

In a furious dive for a fish, his unyielding wings slice the water, tumbling him into the sea. The trauma of his miscalculation is more than a

shock. He is embarrassed because his awkward performance is witnessed, with hysterical laughter, by those on the beach.

"Why are you swimming?" they shout.
"What is the matter with you?"

The dazed eagle prays that a wall of waves will carry him out to sea, away from the ridicule and gossip. He makes no effort to separate himself from the water. He pretends to ignore his hecklers by allowing his spread-out wings to keep him afloat on the calm ocean.

Victor, an old acquaintance, does not laugh. He is concerned for his friend.

"What's the matter with you? I have never
seen you miss a fish. The only time
an eagle swims is when he carries a heavy
fish; and, I do not see a fish!"

"Don't be so hard on me, old friend. The
heaviness is in my heart, and the load is
heavier than I know how to bear."

Victor effortlessly dips into the water and flies to settle on a nearby cypress tree with a shimmering, squirming fish clutched in his talons.

"You have embarrassed yourself this
time," Victor shouts from his perch.

The young Monarch lifts himself out of the
water with his powerful wings and flies to a
branch above his friend. He shakes his wet
feathers. Stretching one leg out in front of him,
he pretends to be oblivious to his surroundings.
He appears content but he is privately anguished. He confesses to Victor:

"I am sad. In an unguarded moment I
wronged a Monarch Butterfly as well as
myself. My ego went soaring too high
upon the wind."

"A Monarch Butterfly!" Victor gasps.
"That is such a lesser creature. Why
do you waste your energy?"

The dejected eagle becomes irate with his old
friend who does not understand what he is trying
to say.

"How can you be so insensitive? I tried
to kill her spirit," he confesses.
"But, when I realized her determination
was stronger than my own, I knew I had
wronged her."

His companion twitters,

> "Your words are like the casting of the
> gull . . . all mixed up."

> "No, dear friend, I am no longer confused.
> For the first time I realize how mistaken
> I've been. Now my thoughts are as clear
> as the beacon light that directs the
> giant birds of man."

> "Bunk!" old Victor scoffs. "I wish I
> could understand you. I really do, but
> I can't believe what's happened to you.
> You're just not the same eagle I have
> hunted with these years."

> "You're right, I'm not the same. But
> have I ever lied to you?"

Victor nods his head in a slow, puzzled way and
replies,

> "No, we have always been honest with each
> other."

Victor moves to another branch of the tree, using
the trunk to shade himself from the sun. He listens

in silence as his young friend continues to ponder his thoughts.

>"I have met another who taught me the magnitude of being honest with myself as well as others. I now have a greater awareness of freedom with no limitations."

Victor laughs at his friend and asks:

>"One butterfly taught you all that?"

The young eagle is sad that Victor does not understand.

>"Oh, dear friend, must you crack the ice to see the water? You don't know how good it feels to be honest and free from the burden of guilt."

>"Honesty?" Victor mumbles.

He snaps his beak and twists his head in a circular motion, then pushes himself from his perch to soar away from his young friend who continues to talk to himself:

>"Honesty is indeed a fulfillment when you believe it and live it. He who knows this is master of himself."

Victor flies back to the tree long enough to share one last bit of wisdom with his friend:

"Maybe so, but I don't know. What I do know is that you had better change direction and stop wasting energy or you will lose yourself in the wind."

The proud young Monarch is hurt and angry. Totally provoked, he spreads his wings and catches the wind. He soars gracefully along the brow of his mountain. Forcing as hard as he can, he climbs into the clouds and disappears from view.

The anger within him subsides as his mind turns to his friend's warning about changing direction. This reminds him that negative thoughts set in motion remain in motion unless countered with a far greater force of positive thought.

The eagle climbs high into the darkened sky. His concentration is so deep that he flies into the swift current of the winds of the jet stream. Deep in thought, he ignores his surroundings and its dangers.

"Why didn't she listen to my heart
instead of the harsh words I spoke? She
could have been more sensitive to my
feelings. After all, she was the intruder. . .
But, perhaps her need for understanding
was greater than mine. Oh, why didn't I
accept her?"

The confused eagle is sorry for sending her away, but it is difficult for him to seek forgiveness. His regret must be acknowledged, for only then will he and the butterfly rise on the wings of giving. He knows, too, that to seek forgiveness, and not be acknowledged, is not unlike a pebble falling into the ocean; the action, once completed, goes unnoticed.

"I will find the butterfly and seek
forgiveness," He promises himself.

The eagle struggles with the increasing velocity of the forceful current. Even thoughts of the butterfly are forced from his mind as he begins to strain and pump his giant wings to do battle with the wind until there is hardly no oxygen left to feed his starving blood. The struggle ends when he exhausts his energy. He grows limp and plummets motionless into the cold whitecapped waters of the breast of the earth.

He awakens to the rising and falling of the heartbeat that surrounds him with the realization that he is blind. His wings suspend him on top of the pounding, swelling waters. The darkness surrounding him is a unique stranger. He feels pain such as he has never known. Echoing deep within his consciousness is the knowledge that he must get to shore.

> "I will survive because my desire to live will create the energy within me. I must survive. I will survive," he promises himself.

> "Because of my will power, I shall become absolute master of myself again, for I will not be counted as a fallen Monarch."

The young eagle must sustain his energy. He must get food. He is not only hampered by the pain wracking his body, but his giant wings are blotting up water. The additional weight makes floating more difficult. He must do something before he sinks.

He rests by floating, and he floats with the occasional movement of his bruised cuffs. The storm that pounded him into the ocean has passed, but the eagle has other threats to his survival. He

realizes his chances of getting back to shore are slim. At any moment he could be snatched from the chilling waters by another predator as vicious as he. He cannot, and will not, allow himself to think such thoughts.

"Positive thoughts, I must be positive.
I will survive to soar again into the
splendor that knows no dimension."

Real darkness surrounds him, the full moon casts moving shadows through the clouds onto the water. Refusing to relent, the eagle draws upon the last strains of energy within him. With great difficulty he keeps his head above the water. And then, almost without warning, he realizes he has collided with something. He is too numb to feel fear. He floats beside the immobile object for an eternity of seconds. In a sudden glorious awakening he realizes he has been guided to the side of a barnacle-covered log. With excruciating pain, he forces his talons deep into its bark. He holds on with all the fierceness he can recall. He clings to the splinters he has loosened with his talons. He pulls himself up onto the raft, shakes the water from his feathers and silently floats on his precarious perch. A great joy befalls him. Now he knows he will have the courage to try to reach the shore. Although his vision has not returned, he can sense land is not far away because he can hear the waves hitting the rocks. It is a sound he knows so well, the familiar sound that greeted him each day in his lair on the side of the craggy cliffs overlooking the peaceful Pacific Ocean.

"Will I ever find my way back home?"

"I will find my way home! he corrects himself.

Comforted by his own reassurances, he remembers the butterfly.

"What was it she said that made me so angry?" he ponders. "She told me that with enthusiasm anything was possible. How could I have been so insensitive to her wisdom?"

Just before the sun appears on the horizon, a pelican joins the eagle. The eagle is startled and starts to lift himself off. The pelican's sympathetic tone reassures the blind bird that he is in no immediate danger.

"Do not be alarmed. I was on my way to the fishing fleet to get the first of their

castings when I noticed your limp wings
and drooping head. Are you hurt?''

''It is kind of you to ask. I am all
right, just lost in a sea of awareness
that has no light.''

The eagle's words confuse the pelican. He cocks
his head to look at the fallen Monarch. He scratches
his beak on the barnacles clinging to the log
but says nothing. The eagle pauses for a long moment,
then continues to confess his agonizing
thoughts.

''When I lost my chosen one, I became
content to dream my life away. Then
another Monarch came my way; she offered
to share her joy with me, but I refused
to acknowledge her. In my search to seek
forgiveness, I followed her into a
strange world, a world I was not
prepared to receive.''

''You are indeed a very strange bird,''
the pelican tells him. ''I will not even
try to understand you. I will pass the
word that you are safe but without vision.''

"There is no need to pass the word. I
no longer have friends, only enemies who
wait on shore to pick my bones. Tell no
one of me."

The injured eagle slips into the water, leaving the
safety of his ocean raft, and swims toward the
roar of the shore.

The punishment of trying to reach land is beyond
proportion to all he has experienced. The
weakness that is in him is more than just pain. He
is a fallen eagle. No longer does he have the
strength to shield himself from the dangers he has
known. The songs do not come from his heart as
they did when he knew no weakness.

He cannot defend himself now. He forces his
wings to move in order to swim the torturous
distance to the shore. He drives his giant cuffs
deep into the choppy water in a purposeful motion. The salt water stings his blurred eyes and his
own splashing chokes him and slows his efforts.
Finally, with a softness he never believed possible, the ocean delivers him onto the sand, and he
knows he is safe for a time. His damaged eyes
burn against the biting particles of sand and salt.
Fingers of wind ripple through his wet feathers as
he lies exhausted in the receding waters. When he

comes to the realization that he is safe, a wave of relief overcomes him and he slips into a peaceful sleep of unconsciousness. In this escape he finds himself considering the inner workings of a cobweb. He sees the intersecting twines of silk as paths of life. Some paths are in a circle, while others lead in a straight line to the light. He imagines himself soaring through the intersecting trails of silk, whole and undiminished.

The eagle tries to determine which path to follow in this image of beauty where life force is enjoyed. He chooses not to go on accepting all that takes place. His awareness is first achieved in the realization of things dreamed. This state of awareness is more than a mere pattern of realization of things sought after. It is his heart and mind unified in a singleness of purpose. Fulfillment is more to him than **just** expectation. It is a moment of awe. Such is that finite twine which moves the puppet beyond self.

In his dream he realizes that the true pattern of behavior is motivated by the whims of forces beyond his awareness. Such whims drive him to panoramas of experiences that are not really known, only dreamed. And yet, dreams confine him by his previous accepted patterns of life.

To be moved on the wings of utmost desire is to know the apex of realization. As the babbling brook sings the song of freedom, knowing no bounds, so do the wings of desire carry him to the zenith of freedom, separating the inner self from the outer self, knowing no dimension of being. The eagle's dream is halted when the incoming tide penetrates his body in an abrupt awakening. He clucks and screeches in response to the sudden inward joy that he is not dead.

He crawls beyond the rim of the tide and allows the sun to warm his wrecked body. As the sun dries his feathers, the heat penetrates his bruised wings. His pain subsides. He realizes he is fortunate to be alive and no longer chooses to follow his old pattern of warring against the way of his mind. He cries to himself:

> "O wretched soul that I have become! Who shall deliver me from this misery?"

The eagle knows it is impossible to fly without vision, so he remains near the water's edge where food is plentiful. His sightless eyes block the stars from his view. Only the sun's heat is his friend. He recovers his strength through its warmth.

The long, lonely days and nights of arduous wandering turn into weeks of seeking. Food is plentiful along the beach. The bald eagle does not require fresh food; that, he reserves for his young. This eagle is a scavenger. His hunger is not for food but for revival. The once brave and fearless Monarch hides in the rocks by day and casts his lone shadow on the deserted beach at night. He is fearful his old enemies will catch him off guard. The sun and his thoughts are all that keep him alive and active.

He recalls long-forgotten experiences from the recesses of his remembrance. He cannot accept his limited condition. He imagines himself soaring on the wind. In that hushed maze of beauty, he acknowledges the limits of his existence. The eagle realizes he has taken the first step on that long journey to climb the 'steps of time.'

His thoughts are shattered by a greeting shouted from a short distance down the beach.

"Hello, my friend!"

The eagle recognizes the voice. It is the pelican that joined him on the ocean raft the day he washed ashore. How long ago that day now seems. Not only has he had to endure the suffering of his

blindness, but the fear of scorn from his enemies has been unbearable. Would that he could commit his spirit into the air, without weakness, knowing no limitations.

The pelican strolls up onto the rocks and peers down at the frayed, desperate eagle.

"Wake up!" he shouts. "I have news for you!"

The awakened eagle shakes his body to rid himself of the unpleasant memories that shrouded him through his convalescence.

"So, you," snarls the eagle,
" are the answer to my prayers?"

The pelican laughs and jumps down from the rock to the side of the eagle.

"You and your fancy language," he teases. "You sent me on a wild goose chase!"

The eagle does not understand what the pelican is trying to say.

"Has your vision failed you, too?" the eagle inquires.

The friendly pelican teases:

> "Of course not. I'm not given to chasing
> geese . . . nor butterflies."

The haggard bird straightens up. His legs stiffen, his feathers compress. His blind eyes flicker and his head twists in a circular motion. The pelican chuckles at the reaction, then continues:

> "I finally tracked down your Monarch, but
> you should have told me she was a Monarch
> Butterfly, not a Monarch of the sky."

The befuddled eagle is filled with a surge of power he has not known since his accident. In his dazed state he confesses:

> "It's true, a butterfly was my motivation
> for survival."

The pelican is again confused by the eagle's vocabulary.

> "I don't understand about 'your motiva-
> tion,' but there is an army of butterflies
> headed this way, and your delightful friend
> is among them. I found her and millions
> like her at their wintering spot."

The news of the butterfly stirs the joyous eagle with renewed hope. No longer lost, he is revived and with purpose. The anticipation of the butterfly creates the desire for freedom within him that he failed to recognize in her.

The eagle departs from his rocky sanctuary to the sun-baked sand,

"I wonder what I will say to the butterfly," he mutters. "I pray we will not meet again on the battlefield of the past. I also wonder which of the forces will be accepted: reason or passion? Shall I allow my reason to direct her passion?

"How can I justify my acceptance of her enthusiasm now?" he questions.

The pelican shrugs. "That's going to be difficult."

"I might be blind," the eagle tells the pelican, "but I can see that the butterfly and I have a singleness of purpose. What do you think? Can 'oneness' be marred by the lack of unity of thought? Does not thought create desire?"

The pelican flaps his wings and shakes his head.
He stands close to the eagle and teases:

"What's all this cackling about 'oneness,'
'awareness,' and 'desire'? You really must
have damaged your brain when you hit the
water. You're a real strange bird all right,
first butterflies, now desire. You're daft
as a looney bird, but I won't tell the
others."

He leans his head to the side and gives the eagle a
gentle nudge with his wing feathers, then flies off.

CHAPTER THREE

Secure that they will be reunited, the eagle becomes concerned about his appearance. He feels unclean and incomplete. Some of his body feathers are awry, and his feet are caked with sand. He moves abruptly, turning left, then right, not quite sure what he should do.

Without warning or reason, the feathers on the back of his neck rise in a puff. A warm tingling sensation races through his body. It stirs every nerve with anticipation. The beautiful butterfly lights on the feathers at the back of the stunned eagle's neck.

"News of you was carried upon the wind,
I heard it, and I'm here."

"Why have you returned? I did not send
for you. I don't need you, go away,"
he thunders.

The butterfly is not surprised by his attitude. After all, this is the same eagle who chased her out of his lair with unprovoked wrath. But, for her to know to do good, and not do it, is a sin. She must help him.

> "I will not stay if you wish to be alone,
> but by now you should know there is a
> destiny between us that makes us one."

The eagle paces among the rocks. He loses his footing and falls onto the sand. He is shaken by this frail, complex creature that has returned to find him broken and humiliated.

> "I don't need your harassment. I have
> enough troubles. What I need is to be able
> to fly again."

The butterfly is not discouraged by his attitude.

> "Oh, dear eagle," she whispers as she
> flutters above his head, "what do we live
> for if it is not to make life less difficult
> for others?"

> "How can you, an ordinary butterfly, help
> me? You might be a Monarch, but I am the
> **eagle**."

The prancing, dancing butterfly has a spirit that is indomitable, not unlike her delicate wings which seem to move about at will. She is determined to lighten the burden of the irascible eagle. She realizes she cannot leave him in such despair. His positive thoughts must be renewed. How can she ignite his desire to activate his own self-will? She must make him want to do what he can do.

"Why do you wish to live for yourself alone? Aloneness is for those who think they have nothing to give," she explains.

"For once you're right, I have nothing to give. I do not wish to be reminded of the past."

He settles down in the warm sand. He spreads his wings in the sunshine for a few moments. In silence he ponders the discussion, then draws his wings into his body.

The butterfly does not relent.

"But you must try," she pleads, "I will help you."

"Nobody can help me," he cries. "Go away and leave me the dignity of suffering in private."

The butterfly's energy dwindles with each moment spent in convincing the stubborn eagle that he can rise up out of his desperation. She wants to teach him that he has the ability to change his thoughts. She wants him to realize that through his mind he can choose cheer instead of depression, confidence instead of fear, love instead of loneliness, and success instead of failure.

"You must stop squandering the precious gift of energy on foolish fear and negative attitudes. Look beyond yourself. Transcend and purify your thoughts. Think!"

The eagle is hurt, but he is afraid to reveal even a hint of his emotional awareness. He tells her to go away, but they are mere words.

Her time left on earth is short. Now she listens to his heart.

The eagle looks about, trying to see the butterfly.

"I am here to the left of you," she whispers. "I will flutter my wings, can you not see them move?"

The eagle turns his body to the left. There is a long moment of silence. He twists his head and jerks it

forward as though he were squinting to take aim
at a fish as he did so long ago.

> "I know it is just my imagination; but,
> I thought for a moment that I saw the
> flickering of a shadow. But that's impos-
> sible. I am blind."

> "You will not be blind for long. You
> must believe you will see again, and
> I want to help you."

In a low whisper, the eagle asks:

> "How do I know I can trust you?"

> "In your mind, I am the least of the
> least, but you can trust me," she assures
> him. "I will guide you home. You cannot
> continue to live as you have."

The eagle is hesitant to accept her offer of
assistance, but he remembers that once before he
rejected her words of friendship. The butterfly
has lightened the heaviness in his heart. He knows
that his spirit will no longer wander upon the
wind. There was a time when he thought he was
complete, needing no thing. Now, out of his renewed enthusiasm, he brings himself to say,

"I will allow you to guide me, but it
will be **my** wings that carry us
to **my** mountain."

The butterfly looks at him in a curious manner
and asks:

"You mean to your nest?"

"No," he says, "just guide me back to
my mountain. There I will find my own way.
You are not permitted, if you recall."

The butterfly winces at his cutting remark, but
continues to maintain her composure.

"Oh, dear blind eagle, you had knowledge
when we first met, but by now I had hoped
you would have risen to a higher arena of
wisdom."

The eagle pretends to ignore her statement.

"Arenas are for the goring of the bulls
and the sacrificing of gladiators,"
he snaps.

The butterfly is saddened by his attitude. She cannot penetrate the protective wall in which his

emotions are sealed. Even though her own life is almost spent, she continues to peel away at the layers.

> "Dear friend," she pleads, "can you
> still not see that arenas are where we
> arrive when we realize the true path of
> awareness? As our mind grows, we advance
> step by step, to a higher plane."

The eagle is haunted by her determination to reach deep into the very core of his being. How he wishes he could cry out to her, as she did to him when they first met in his tree. She sought understanding then; but, he did not give understanding. Now she seeks desperately to ignite his awareness; but, he cannot bring himself to share his secrets, not even with her.

> "I trust you to guide me to my mountain,
> but I will not listen to your pearls of
> wisdom along the way."

In spite of his attitude, the butterfly senses a semblance of his yielding. She realizes that in their mutual need, they have reached an awareness of one spirit, one mind, striving together.

"I can only guide you with my spirit; but,
alas, my time is short."

The eagle stands proud and straight once again.
His head rotates in a circular motion as he asks,

"What do you mean, 'your time is short'?"

The butterfly, wings sealed together as one,
rests on a rock near him.

"Never mind, let us be on our way,"
is her swift response.

The moment is an awkward one for the eagle. He
wishes to stretch his wings and lift himself up into
the air, but he hesitates.

"Don't be in such a hurry. Your enthusiasm
is really something, little butterfly, but
the greatest eagle in the world would not
attempt to fly without light."

The butterfly is quick to assure him that she will
guide the way. The eagle is just as quick to remind
her that his speed is much greater than hers. It is
he who finally resolves the problem.

"Oh, you dull creature, just squeeze under
the feathers on my neck, they will protect
you from the wind; and, you can guide me
away from the trees and hilltops."

She does just as he orders. She brings her wings
together in a perpindicular line with her body and
forces her tiny feet deep into the furry white
feathers on his neck. A joyous feeling overcomes
her as the giant bird pushes himself away from
his rocky retreat into the wind.

The butterfly draws upon the last of her wisdom to
give him encouragement.

"Keep your wings energized," she urges.
"Keep the blood circulating. Draw your
strength from the air. Your renewed energy
will clear your head."

"Didn't I ask you not to privilege me
with your insight?" He jerks his neck
as he speaks.

His movements make it almost impossible for her
to hang on.

After a few moments of silent flight, the eagle
begins to force his wings to move faster and
stronger. His breathing becomes consistent with

the rhythm of his body movements. The butterfly fans her wings to the same rhythm. They are partners in the same pattern. The response to her guidance is so electrifying that he realizes a surge of power he has not known for a long time. Once more he wills the attitude he had forgotten . . . to soar without dimension.

The butterfly shares his joy. She tries not to detract from his moment of glory.

"Now that you are no longer deprived of energy, are you not once more master of yourself?"

"You dare to ask, to know?" he teases.

The delicate butterfly is hurt by his words, the same words she used so long ago. Her response is one of anguished silence. To escape the hurt and pain, she focuses her mind on a higher arena of thought.

"The most beautiful quality of true friendship is to understand and to be understood."

She pauses for a moment, then continues.

"You will never understand me, for we
never know the true value of friendship
while our friends are with us. We are too
sensitive to their faults. It is when we
lose them that we see their virtues,"
she explains.

Her words cut through his toughened shell like an
arrow slicing the bark of a log. His entire body
shakes in a violent shiver at their meaning. She
has finally succeeded in chipping a chunk of the
emotional facade from his spirit. In quick defense
to his shattered ego, he demands:

"Are we not friends? When you speak of
friendship, what do you mean? Is there a
difference between friendship and oneness?"

Now it is the butterfly that is caught off guard by
his probing question. She thinks for a long moment before she attempts to answer. The eagle
continues to fly in a rhythm of movements. The
butterfly's well-chosen words mesmerize the
thoughts of the rejuvenated Monarch:

"Oneness is a form of intelligence above
language. It is more than friendship. It
is more than faith. Oneness is freedom of
thought, bound by awareness of the light,
in quest of life."

The eagle allows himself to drift aimlessly in order to concentrate on the pureness of her words.

"Do you mean," he asks, "that if you and I think alike, we would be more than friends, we would know oneness?"

The butterfly laughs.

"No," she replies, "that would be no more than thinking alike."

Well, I certainly don't think like you think," he teases.

She pays no attention. She continues:

"We would experience oneness when our hearts and minds are perfectly joined in spirit and awareness," she explains.

The eagle concentrates so completely on the butterfly's words that he develops a speed so great he automatically blinks his eyes to protect them from the rushing wind.

"Why do you place more importance on the spiritual than the physical?" the eagle wants to know. "In my domain it is the

one who catches the biggest fish, has the largest nest, and the eagle who flies the highest who is the success.''

The butterfly buries her head deep into the fur of his neck. She is at a loss for words. She feels as though she has failed. She has failed herself, for her energy is spent. That she failed him is even a heavier blow to her spirit.

"You have not listened to my words," she cries. "You are truly a lost soul, and I have failed you."

"Oh, my little friend, you haven't failed me, nor have I failed you. Are we not taking the impossible flight together?"

The eagle's wing movements gain momentum. His eyes remain closed. The tormented butterfly relaxes her emotional control and sobs silently into his furry neck.

"Will you stop that?! Stealing a ride with me like a parasite is one thing, but I will not have you soaking my fluffy white neck feathers with your tears!"

The eagle opens his eyes and twists his neck in an effort to shake his feathers. But as he does, he **sees** the delicate creature half hidden in his feathers desperately holding on to the last moments of her time. The sight of her so close to him delays the reaction to his regained vision. He forgets about her the moment he realizes he can see. It hits him with great force.

> "I can see! I can see!" he cries over
> and over.

The excited eagle pulls upward into a steep climb. The butterfly does not make a sound.

> "Hang on, butterfly, now I'm going to show
> you **real** oneness!"

He continues to climb with power, then into a left wing stall and a violent roll into a vertical dive. His wings half closed, he pretends to spot a target, pulling up just short of the tree tops.

> "How's that for fulfillment?" he
> joyfully teases his weary passenger.

> "I'm so weak and thirsty, I don't think
> I can make it to your mountain," she
> cries.

"Oh ye of little faith, we're here,"
he boasts.

He circles above his lair in silent acknowledge-
ment of his return. Without a word of warning to
his passenger, he folds his wings and drops in a
dive toward his nest. He levels out and settles on
a nearby rock not far from his tree. She flutters
away from his neck. Her wings no longer flash
in the fan-like movement of her youth. The eagle
looks at her but he does not see the change that
has taken place.

She leaves the eagle and flutters to a nearby
stream to linger by the water. She is sad because
the eagle has not achieved awareness.

The eagle watches her wings grow still as he
swoops down to her side. He is steeled at the
realization that her time was indeed short, too
short. He delicately picks her up with his beak and
lifts off to soar above his lair for an infinite moment. He descends to the center of his nest, still
holding her in his beak. He places her beside him
so tenderly that she seems like the softest cloud
silk. He roots at his nest to prepare a place for her
in his mansion. He drives his great talons deep into the side of his lair, removing twigs and leaves

to form a hole. He pulls feathers from his own
body to prepare her coffer. As though she were a
piece of cobweb, he lays her delicately into the
center of his sunken vault. He covers her with
more of his own feathers, twigs and leaves, en-
tombing her forever in his heart and dreams.

The eagle's eyes are moist. His words once more
lost on the wind:

> "There is a silence where hath been only
> sounds. There is a sound where no sound
> may be; and yet, your presence shall
> thunder forever.

> "It was life in quest of life you made
> me aware of, but you wrapped it in the
> web of oneness, and bound it with the
> freedom of eternal light.

> "Oh, butterfly, please know that from
> this acceptance you will realize the
> worth of your pain. Because you filled
> my soul, we soared together into the
> splendor of the light to find the utmost."

Book Design by Dawn Ellen Moline

Printed by Blake Printery